REAL LIFE
MATH: BLUE
LEVEL

REAL LIFE
MATH

treasure
in the
JUNGLE

Wendy Clemson and Frances Clemson

Ticktock

This library edition published in 2014 by Ticktock
First published in the USA in 2013 by Ticktock,
an imprint of Octopus Publishing Group Ltd

Distributed by Black Rabbit Books
P.O. Box 3263, Mankato, MN 56002

Cataloging-in-Publication Data is available from the Library of Congress
ISBN 978 1 78325 186 5

Printed and bound in China

1 3 5 7 9 10 8 6 4 2

Picture Credits
t=top, b=bottom, c=center, l=left, r=right, f=far
Amazon-Images/Alamy: 2, 19t. Wolfgang Kaehler/Alamy: 11. Yann Arthus-Bertrand/Corbis: 29. e.t. archive: 1.
Shutterstock: front cover, 3c, 3fl, 4tl, 4tr, 4bl, 4br, 5, 7, 8, 9, 10, 13, 14, 15, 16t, 16c, 16b,
17t, 17b, 18, 19b, 20, 21, 22, 23, 24-25, 27, 30, 31b, 31t, 32.
Werner Forman Archive: 6b. TickTock archive: 6t
BFL e.t. archive. Back cover: TL and BR Shutterstock.

Every effort has been made to trace the copyright holders, and we apologize in advance for any unintentional omissions.
We would be pleased to insert the appropriate acknowledgement in any subsequent edition of this publication.

Contents

MATH SKILLS COVERED IN THIS BOOK:

Numbers and the number system
Rounding: pp. 6–7
Place value: pp. 8–9
Odds and evens: pp. 16–17
Putting numbers in order: pp. 18–19
Fractions: pp. 24–25

Shape, space, and measurements
Telling Time: pp. 8–9
Flat shapes: pp. 10–11
Compass N, S, E, and W: pp. 12–13
Miles: pp. 12–13
Measuring length: pp. 14–15
Estimates: pp. 18–19
Measuring with a ruler: pp. 20–21
Solid shapes: pp. 22–23
Angles: pp. 28–29

Organizing data
Venn diagram (sorting): pp. 10–11
Meaning of signs +. –, x: pp. 16–17
Picture graph: pp. 26–27

Problem solving
Predicting patterns: pp. 24–25

Mental calculations
Groups of 10: p. 6
Addition, subtraction, and multiplication: pp. 17, 19, 21
Counting and difference: p. 18

Supports math standards for ages 8+

Be an Explorer

You are an explorer. You travel all over the world. Explorers find amazing places that very few people have ever seen. Today you are going on an exciting adventure to search for hidden treasure. If you find some treasure, you will give it to a museum so that everyone can see it!

Being an explorer can be dangerous, but it can also be great fun!

Explorers climb mountains and trek through jungles.

Sometimes explorers see unusual wild animals!

Explorers find treasures and ancient ruins that tell us about the past.

They sometimes have to camp in very hot or cold places.

But did you know that explorers sometimes have to use math?

4

In this book you will find lots of number puzzles that explorers have to solve to help them find out about secret places and treasures. You will also get the chance to answer lots of number questions about the things you see.

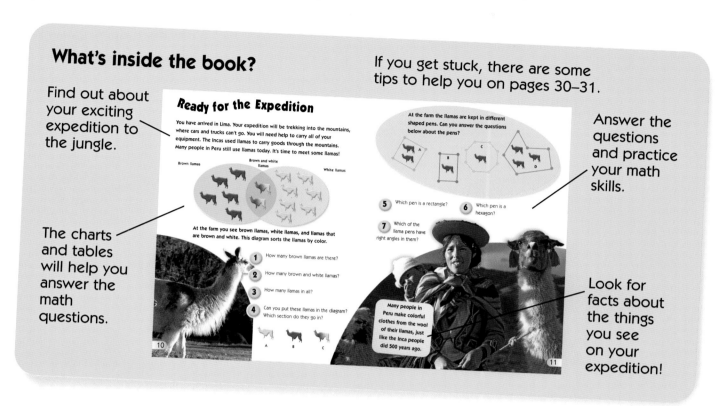

What's inside the book?

Find out about your exciting expedition to the jungle.

The charts and tables will help you answer the math questions.

If you get stuck, there are some tips to help you on pages 30–31.

Answer the questions and practice your math skills.

Look for facts about the things you see on your expedition!

Ready for the Expedition

You have arrived in Lima. Your expedition will be trekking into the mountains, where cars and trucks can't go. You will need help to carry all of your equipment. The Incas used llamas to carry goods through the mountains. Many people in Peru still use llamas today. It's time to meet some llamas!

Brown llamas   Brown and white llamas   White llamas

At the farm you see brown llamas, white llamas, and llamas that are brown and white. This diagram sorts the llamas by color.

1. How many brown llamas are there?
2. How many brown and white llamas?
3. How many llamas in all?
4. Can you put these llamas in the diagram? Which section do they go in?

A   B   C

At the farm the llamas are kept in different shaped pens. Can you answer the questions below about the pens?

A   B   C   D

5. Which pen is a rectangle?
6. Which pen is a hexagon?
7. Which of the llama pens have right angles in them?

Many people in Peru make colorful clothes from the wool of their llamas, just like the Inca people did 500 years ago.

10   11

Are you ready to be an explorer?

You will need paper, a pencil, and a ruler, and don't forget to bring your equipment! Let's go...

Looking for Treasure!

You are going on a trip to Peru, a country in South America. On your adventure you will climb mountains and explore thick, dark jungle. You will see ruins and lots of unusual animals. If you are lucky, you hope to find Inca treasure hidden in the jungle to give to a museum in Peru!

The Inca people lived in Peru about 500 years ago. This is an Inca picture of ten warriors.

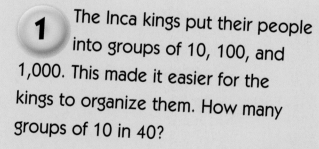

1 The Inca kings put their people into groups of 10, 100, and 1,000. This made it easier for the kings to organize them. How many groups of 10 in 40?

2 How many groups of 10 are there in 110?

3 If you put 82 people into groups of 10, how many groups of 10 will there be?

4 How many people will be left over?

This is a gold Inca mask. The Incas had lots of gold and silver treasure.

5 Round each of these numbers to the nearest 10:
33   65   78   40   96

6 Which of these numbers have a 5 in the hundreds place:
35   579   56   1,509   1,536

Machu Picchu was built around 1440. It was a sacred place high up in the Andes Mountains.

Off to Peru

You are leading a team of explorers. The members of your team are coming from all over the world. Some of them have a long plane journey to reach Peru. You will meet the other explorers in Lima, the capital city of Peru.

FLIGHT TIMES TO LIMA

Leaving from		Going to	Time it will take
London	United Kingdom	Lima, Peru	17 hours
Washington, D.C.	United States	Lima, Peru	11 hours
Moscow	Russia	Lima, Peru	21 hours
Mexico City	Mexico	Lima, Peru	6 hours
Nairobi	Kenya	Lima, Peru	29 hours

1 Look at the flight times chart. How long does it take to get from Washington, D.C., to Lima?

2 How long does it take to get from Moscow to Lima?

3 Which journey takes the least time?

4 Which journey takes longer than a day?

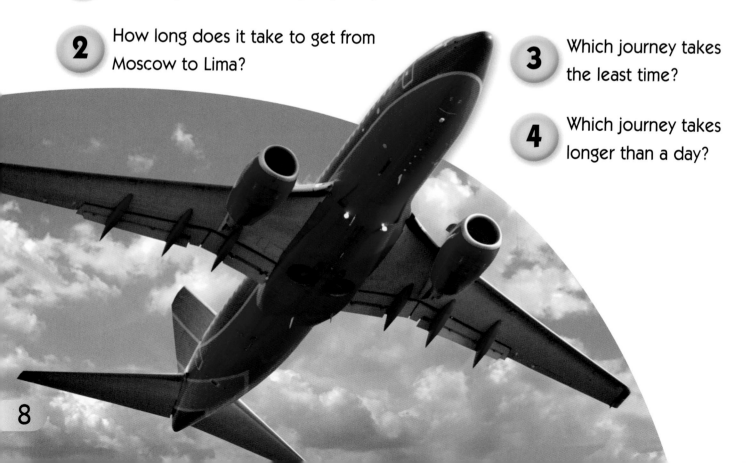

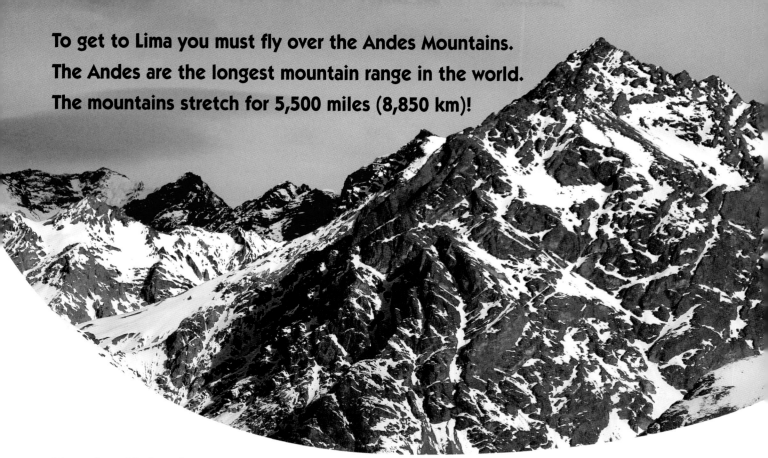

To get to Lima you must fly over the Andes Mountains. The Andes are the longest mountain range in the world. The mountains stretch for 5,500 miles (8,850 km)!

Use the flight times chart to answer the questions on this page.

5 If you leave Washington, D.C., at 12:00, which clock shows your arrival time?

A

B

C
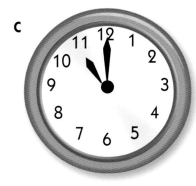

6 If an explorer leaves Mexico City at 3:00, which clock shows his arrival time?

A

B

C

9

Ready for the Expedition

You have arrived in Lima. Your expedition will be trekking into the mountains, where cars and trucks can't go. You will need help to carry all of your equipment. The Incas used llamas to carry goods through the mountains. Many people in Peru still use llamas today. It's time to meet some llamas!

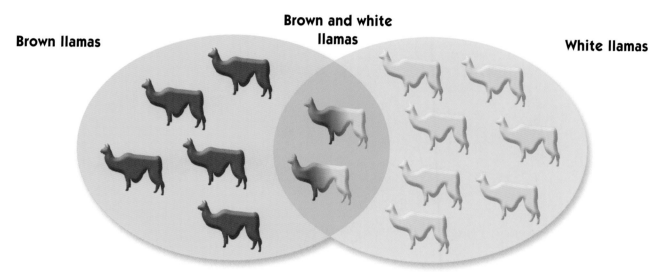

Brown llamas

Brown and white llamas

White llamas

At the farm you see brown llamas, white llamas, and llamas that are brown and white. This diagram sorts the llamas by color.

1 How many brown llamas are there?

2 How many brown and white llamas?

3 How many llamas in all?

4 Can you put these llamas in the diagram? Which section do they go in?

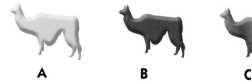

A   B   C

At the farm the llamas are kept in different shaped pens. Can you answer the questions below about the pens?

A

B

C

D

5 Which pen is a rectangle?

6 Which pen is a hexagon?

7 Which of the llama pens have right angles in them?

Many people in Peru make colorful clothes from the wool of their llamas, just like the Inca people did 500 years ago.

High in the Mountains

Being an explorer can be very tough! You are trekking along rocky mountain roads. When you are high up in the mountains, the air is thinner. This makes it hard to breathe, and it can make you feel sick! Thankfully you planned your trip for May, when it is not too hot or too cold in Peru.

1 Look at the months of the year. Can you put them in the right order?

2 If the expedition lasts until the end of May, what month will it be when you go home?

MONTHS OF THE YEAR

May	April	September
June	August	January
July	October	November
February	December	March

WOW! You have just spotted a condor. The condor is one of the biggest birds in the world. These giant birds live high in the Andes Mountains.

Condors don't flap their wings very often. Instead they glide on the air currents as they look for food.

The condor's wings measure 10 feet (3.04 m) from tip to tip.

3 How many inches in one foot?

4 How many inches in half a foot?

5 How many inches (cm) in 3 feet (.91 m)?

6 Is ¼ foot more or less than 4 inches?

15

Into the Jungle

You are following the treasure map into the jungle. Explorers take photographs and make notes about everything they see on an expedition. The jungle is full of unusual animals to look out for. What's that noise? It's a fierce, fast big cat called a jaguar!

1 Jaguars are covered in spots. This makes it hard for other animals to see them when the jaguars are hunting in the shady jungle. Which of the three jaguars below has an odd number of spots?

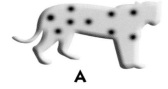
A

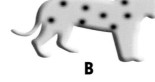
B

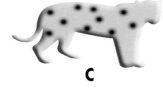
C

2 Which have even numbers of spots?

3 Which one has the fewest spots?

4 Which jaguar has the most spots?

5 Is 3 an odd or an even number?

6 Everywhere you look in the jungle you see little squirrel monkeys. How many can you count on these pages?

Squirrel monkeys live in groups called troops. There are normally 40 to 50 monkeys in one troop. But sometimes there can be 200!

7 Now try these monkey puzzles!

A 2 monkeys + 2 monkeys + 2 monkeys

B 3 x 2 monkeys

C 2 monkeys + 6 monkeys

D 4 monkeys – 2 monkeys

E 2 x 2 monkeys

On the Jungle Floor

On the ground there are thousands of tiny insects and jungle creatures. Look – leafcutter ants! The ants are collecting pieces of leaf and taking them back to their nest. They use the leaves to make a special ant food.

Leafcutter ants can carry pieces of leaf that weigh 20 times their own body weight.

1 Look at the group of leafcutter ants in the box. Estimate how many there are and write it down. Now count the ants. What is the difference between your estimate and the actual number of ants?

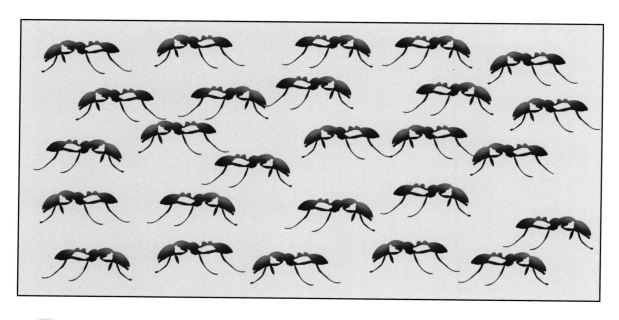

2 How many ants are there rounded to the nearest ten?

You spot a tiny poison dart frog. These frogs have deadly poisonous skin that stops snakes and big spiders eating them!

This poison dart frog is only a half an inch long.

Poison dart frogs come in lots of different colors. Try these frog additions:

3 🐸🐸🐸🐸 + 🐸🐸🐸

4 🐸🐸🐸 + 🐸🐸🐸🐸🐸🐸

5 🐸🐸🐸🐸🐸🐸 + 🐸🐸🐸🐸🐸 + 🐸🐸🐸

6 Millipedes live in the jungle, too. "Millipede" means "1,000 feet," but most millipedes have only between 80 and 400 feet. Which of these numbers are between 80 and 400?

66	81
42	300
93	88
410	100

Jungle Butterflies and Birds

You have now been trekking through the jungle for five days! You walk for about 10 miles every day. Your explorer's notebook is filling up with notes about exciting jungle creatures!

EXPLORER'S NOTEBOOK

Jungle creatures	Number spotted
Jaguars	3
Blue poison dart frogs	10
Millipedes	9
Blue morpho butterflies	16
Red poison dart frogs	22

1 Look at the explorer's notebook. How many millipedes have you seen?

2 Which creature have you seen 16 of?

3 How many poison dart frogs have you seen in all?

4 This is a blue morpho butterfly. This giant butterfly lives in the jungles of South America. Use your ruler to measure the butterfly's wingspan. How many inches does the butterfly measure?

5 You spot a toucan up in the trees. Its huge orange beak is 8 inches (20.32 cm) long. Its body is 25 inches (63.5 cm) long. Can you do these puzzles using 8 and 25?

25 + 8

8 + 8

25 – 8

25 + 25

Toucans are not very good at flying. They hop from tree branch to tree branch!

Discovering the Temple

Suddenly through the thick trees and bushes you spot the ruins of a building. The map was right! You have found an Inca temple. The Incas had lots of different gods, including a sun god. They built temples as special places to make their sun god happy.

The Incas did not have cement to glue stones together. Their walls were built with stones that fit together well.

1 Which of these shapes would be good for building?

 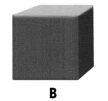 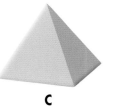 

A   B   C   D

2 Can you match these names to the shapes?

Cylinder   Cube   Sphere   Pyramid

These bricks will be used to build a large triangle shape. Here are the bottom two rows.

3 How many bricks should be in the next row up? How many bricks in the row after that?

4 How many bricks will be at the top of the triangle?

5 Now try this brick pattern. A wall has **30 bricks**, then **25 bricks**, then **20 bricks**. What comes next?

23

Inside the Temple

The Incas' kingdom measured about 3,000 miles (4.827 km) from one end to the other. The land was divided into four parts and named "Tawantinsuyu." This Inca word means "land of the four quarters." You decide to split up your team of explorers into four groups to explore the temple.

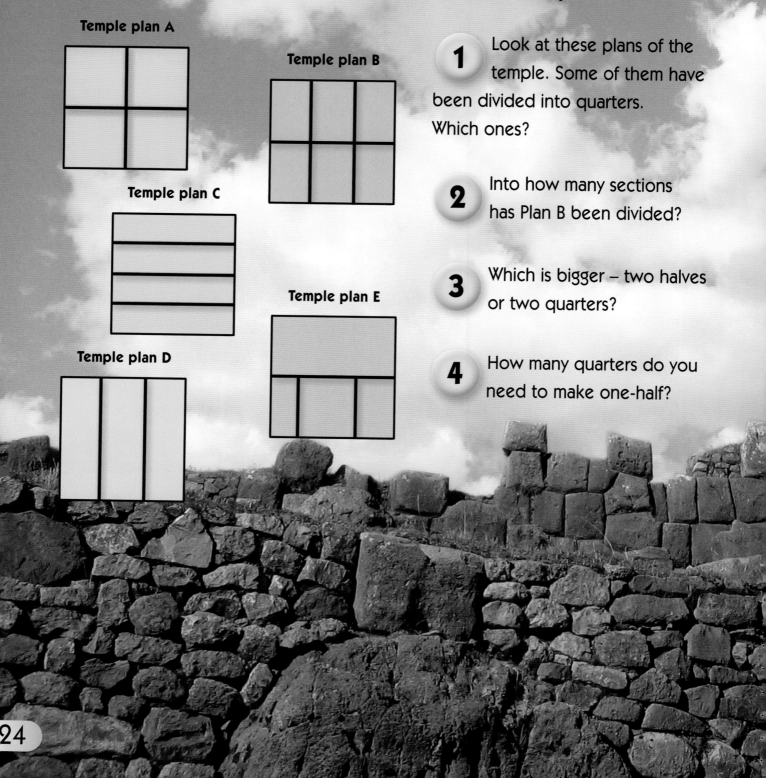

Temple plan A

Temple plan B

Temple plan C

Temple plan E

Temple plan D

1 Look at these plans of the temple. Some of them have been divided into quarters. Which ones?

2 Into how many sections has Plan B been divided?

3 Which is bigger – two halves or two quarters?

4 How many quarters do you need to make one-half?

There is no writing on the walls of the temple. The Inca people did not know how to write. Instead of writing they tied knots in pieces of string. Different numbers of knots gave different messages.

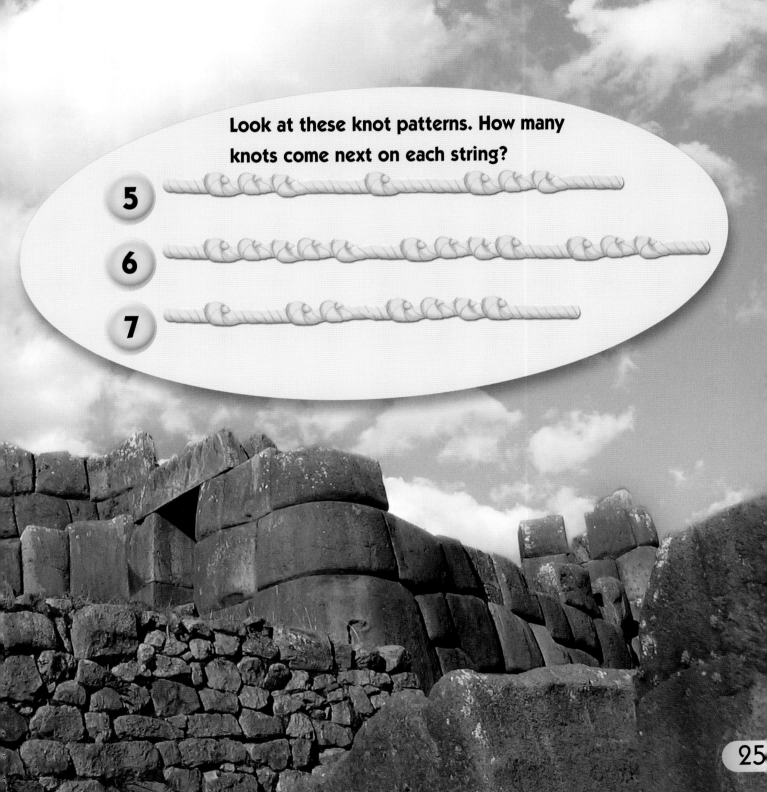

Look at these knot patterns. How many knots come next on each string?

5

6

7

Temple Treasures

There are lots of wonderful treasures in the temple. The Inca kings were very rich. Their people made things from gold and silver dug out of the ground. They used these metals plus copper and bronze, along with stone, pottery, and wood. They made statues, drinking and cooking pots, and jewelry.

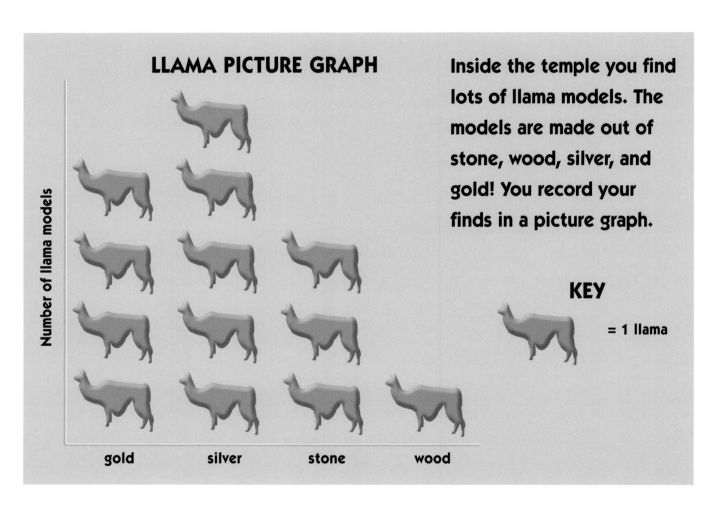

LLAMA PICTURE GRAPH

Number of llama models

gold   silver   stone   wood

Inside the temple you find lots of llama models. The models are made out of stone, wood, silver, and gold! You record your finds in a picture graph.

KEY

= 1 llama

Use the picture graph to answer these questions:

1 How many gold llama models are there?

2 How many more silver llamas than gold llamas?

3 How many more gold llamas than wood llamas?

4 How many llama models did you find in all?

The llamas will have lots of exciting things to carry back to the museum in Lima. They take a rest in the temple ruins!

The Inca's sun god was called Inti and they had a moon god called Quilla. You find lots of model suns and moons in the temple. How many models altogether?

5 You need to pack the models up into boxes of ten. How many boxes will you need?

6 The sun and moon models weigh 2 pounds (.9 kg) each. If a llama can carry 20 pounds (9 kg) on its back, how many llamas do you need to carry the sun and moon models?

Patterns and Pictures

The Incas liked to use patterns, squares, and right angles to decorate their things. On the way home from your expedition, you will fly over some giant pictures and patterns called the Nazca lines. They were drawn in the desert sand by people who lived in Peru 2,000 years ago!

1 We call this a checkerboard pattern. The Incas used it a lot. What numbers would you find in the bottom row of the checkerboard?

2 Would the numbers below be on red or yellow squares?

8   11   17   20

3 Numbers in the 2x table all fall on the same color square. Is that red or yellow?

This is an Inca pattern called a "tocapus." These patterns are found on material. The Incas were very good at weaving.

4 Look at these patterns. Trace the outside of each shape with your finger. How many right angles do you move through?

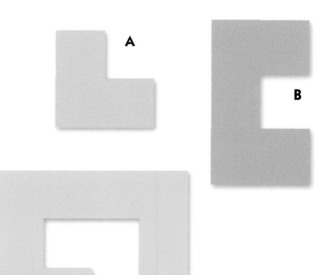

A

B

C

The Nazca drawings include animals, insects, birds, and patterns. As your plane flies over a giant spider drawing, you can see it from different directions.

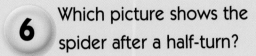

Look at the spider. Your plane is going around clockwise.

A

B

C

5 Which picture shows the spider after a quarter-turn?

6 Which picture shows the spider after a half-turn?

This Nazca spider is 130 feet long! It is just one of the amazing things you have seen on your expedition in Peru!

Tips and Help

PAGES 6–7

Rounding – When we round a number to the nearest ten, we make a number ending in 5, 6, 7, 8, or 9 bigger and numbers ending in 1, 2, 3, or 4 smaller. So 33 rounded to the nearest ten is 30, whereas 65 becomes 70 because it is rounded up.

Place value – We use only ten symbols to write all numbers. The "place" of each symbol gives it "value." For example, 579 has a 5 in the hundreds place, a 7 in the tens place, and a 9 in the ones place, and so we read this number as five hundred and seventy nine.

PAGES 8–9

Telling time – The little hand points to the hour. The big hand points to the minutes. When the little hand is on 3 and the big hand is on 12, the time is three o'clock (3:00).

PAGES 10–11

Sorting – This is called a Venn diagram. It shows a set of brown llamas and white llamas. The sets overlap so that the llamas that are mixed (both brown and white) are in the brown set and the white set.

Flat shapes – Counting the sides is necessary in naming flat shapes. A hexagon has six sides, an octagon eight sides, a rectangle four sides (opposite sides match in length) and four right angles, and a square four sides of equal length and four right angles.

PAGES 12–13

Compass N, S, E, and W – (north, south, east, and west) are called the points of the compass. A compass shows which direction is north. It can help us find our way.

Mile – One mile is 5,280 feet (8,498 km).

PAGES 14–15

Month – There are 12 months in a year.

Measuring length – There are 12 inches (30.48 cm) in one foot.

PAGES 16–17

Odds and evens – Even numbers are in the pattern of counting by twos: 2 4 6 8 and so on. Odd numbers are those that are not even: 1 3 5 7 9 and so on.

Solving problems – Remember that + means add, – means subtract, x means multiply.

PAGES 18–19

Estimate – An estimate can be made when we look at all the information we have and decide what an answer is likely to be. It is very important in mathematics as we can judge whether an answer we have is probably the correct one.

Putting numbers in order – To put these numbers in order starting with the lowest number, try looking at the numbers that are just "tens" and "ones" first. 42 has the fewest tens and so this is the lowest number. When you have all the tens and ones in order, look for the number with the fewest "hundreds" and so on. Then look at your number line and mark where 80 and 400 come. The numbers between 80 and 400 are the answers.

PAGES 20–21

Measuring with a ruler – To measure the width, be sure the zero, or left, edge of the ruler lines up with the end of the left-pointing arrow. The number where the right-pointing arrow ends is the wingspan of the butterfly.

PAGES 22–23

Solid shapes – A sphere is a perfectly round shape. A cube has 6 square faces and 8 corners. A pyramid has a square base, 4 faces that are triangles, and it comes to a "point" called the apex. A cylinder has 1 flat side that wraps around and joins to the 2 identical circles on the end.

PAGES 24–25

Fractions – A fraction is part of a whole. When we share or cut something into four equal parts, each is ¼ (one-fourth). If it is cut into two equal parts, each part is the fraction ½ (one-half).

Predicting patterns – When we work out how a pattern would continue, we are predicting (deciding what will happen). Count the knots, look for a pattern, and then imagine that the same pattern goes on across the page.

PAGES 28–29

Right angle – As you fly in a circle over the Nazca spider, you see the spider from different directions. The spider seems to make quarter-turns. Each quarter-turn forms a right angle. A right angle is often shown like this:

A quarter-turn – There are four quarter-turns in one complete turn, or circle. Each quarter-turn makes a right angle.

PAGES 26–27

Picture graph – This is a graph in which a picture is used as a symbol for information. In this picture graph, a llama shape means 1 llama.

Answers

PAGES 6–7

1 4
2 11
3 8 groups
4 2 people left over
5 30 70 80 40 100
6 579, 1,509, and 1,536

PAGES 8–9

1 11 hours
2 21 hours
3 Mexico City to Lima
4 Nairobi to Lima
5 Clock C
6 Clock A

PAGES 10–11

1 5 brown llamas
2 2 brown and white llamas
3 14 llamas
4 A - white llamas
   B - brown llamas
   C - brown and white llamas
5 B
6 D
7 A and B

PAGES 12–13

1 true
2 false
3 true
4 mountains
5 jungle
6 temple
7 inches
8 miles

PAGES 14–15

1 January, February, March, April, May, June, July, August, September, October, November, December
2 June
3 12 inches
4 6 inches
5 36 inches
6 less than 4 inches

PAGES 16–17

1 A
2 B and C
3 B
4 C
5 odd number
6 8 squirrel monkeys
7 A - 6 monkeys
   B - 6 monkeys
   C - 8 monkeys
   D - 2 monkeys
   E - 4 monkeys

PAGES 18–19

1 there are 26 ants in the box
2 30 ants
3 7 frogs
4 9 frogs
5 13 frogs
6 81, 88, 93, 100, and 300

PAGES 20–21

1 9 millipedes
2 blue morpho butterflies
3 32 poison dart frogs
4 6 inches
5 25 + 8 = 33
   8 + 8 = 16
   25 − 8 = 17
   25 + 25 = 50

PAGES 22–23

1 B
2 A - sphere
   B - cube
   C - pyramid
   D - cylinder
3 3 bricks and then 2 bricks
4 1 brick
5 15 bricks

PAGES 24–25

1 Plan A and Plan C
2 6 sections
3 2 halves
4 2 quarters
5 1 knot
6 2 knots
7 8 knots

PAGES 26–27

1 4 gold llamas
2 1
3 3
4 13 llama models
5 3 boxes
6 3 llamas

PAGES 28–29

1 21, 22, 23, 24, and 25
2 8 = yellow square
   11 = red square
   17 = red square
   20 = yellow square
3 yellow squares
4 A = 6 right angles
   B = 8 right angles
   C = 8 right angles
5 B
6 A